Marco Simonelli

I0517723

WILL

Shakespearian Sonnets

TRANSLATED AND INTRODUCED BY
HOYT ROGERS

SPUYTEN DUYVIL

NEW YORK CITY

© 2024 Marco Simonelli
Translation © 2024 Hoyt Rogers
ISBN 978-1-963908-31-2

Library of Congress Control Number: 2024944457

INTRODUCTION

Marco Simonelli was born in Florence, where he lives to this day; though still in his forties, he has already published a dozen books of verse. His work has figured widely in periodicals, anthologies, and literary festivals; it has been translated into English, French, and German. Some of his titles—*Good Manners* (2018), *Splatter Love Poems* (2015), and *The Lobster's Complaint* (also 2015)—reveal the mordant wit for which he is known. But this does not preclude a serious vein, poignantly felt in one of his most recent books, *Anxious Litany*: a subtle analysis of depression, the work draws on such classic authors as Tasso, Leopardi, and Pascoli.

Far more light-heartedly, Simonelli's *Will: 24 Sonnets* (2009) pays homage to Shakespeare's sonnets, giving them a modern Tuscan twist. As he points out in his brief prologue, the English poet often makes a pun on his own nickname, "Will" (for example, in sonnets 135 and 136). The word implies many meanings, from strong determination to Elizabethan slang for the male organ, and from lustiness in general to a formal legal testament. But Simonelli underlines a connotation that would not immediately occur to an English-speaker: the ubiquitous role of "will" as an auxiliary verb in the future tense—that horizon of uncertainty which leaves us all in a state of flux.

Simonelli reprises many of Shakespeare's themes, often shared by the Petrarchist tradition as a whole, such as the "sleepless lover" motif of sonnet 2. He also adopts the rhyme-scheme of the English sonnet; the only exceptions are 5 and 24, but even those conclude with the hallmark couplet. Instead of contorting his lines to the brink of the unreadable, I have rendered them in blank verse or iambic tetrameter. But I should point out that Simonelli's rhymes are ingenious, and that he employs them brilliantly in several of his other books. In transposing his sonnets, I came across only one semantic anomaly. In sonnet 16, he combines the word for "pencil" with a phrase about flowing ink. He tells me that this must be an instinctive memory of his first attempts at poetry, when as a child he wrote everything with a pencil. But he agreed that given the context, I should translate the term as "pen" for clarity's sake. Another quirk is the coinage of "musi" in sonnet 18, the "masculine muses" of his fantasies.

Like Shakespeare's sonnets, those of Simonelli are devoted to two distinct lovers; both are male, whereas Shakespeare's are traditionally known as the "fair youth" and the "dark lady." The English sonneteer depicts himself as an older man, which adds the pathos of passing time to some of his most moving poems, such as 71, 72, and 73; Simonelli and his lovers seem to belong to the same age-group. While the young man occupies the lion's share of the English sequence, the Italian sonnets are split more evenly between the "somber" and "sunny" paramours. The "dark lady" only comes to the fore in the latter part of Shakespeare's cycle, whereas the tenebrous lover occupies the first half of Simonelli's sonnets. Number 12 serves as the "envoy" or farewell, much like Shakespeare's dismissal of the "lovely boy" in his lopped-off sonnet 126. Both the youth and the lady bear the brunt of the anti-Petrarchist motifs current in Shakespeare's time—a natural reaction to two and a half centuries of etherealizing the beloved, from Petrarch's Laura to Du Bellay's Olive to Sidney's Stella. He shoots a few arrows at the foolish young man, but he truly empties his quiver on their shared love, the treacherous lady. Here's another parting of ways: in Shakespeare, the poet's lovers become lovers in turn, much to his dismay, while Simonelli keeps his paramours separate. Perhaps because of the much shorter compass of *Will*—24 sonnets to Shakespeare's 154—the nebulous "story line" of Shakespeare's cycle is replaced by a crystal-clear progression in Simonelli's. If Shakespeare records a slow decline from worship to disappointment, and from fondness to resentment, Simonelli traces an upward arc from frustration to fulfillment, and from discontent to conjugal bliss.

Will opens with four sonnets that outline the poet's routine before meeting up with his two successive boyfriends. He pursues an endless round of men, whom he imagines as reflections of himself; the sex is casual, ardent, and short-lived. Over time, his promiscuity seems to offer him little satisfaction, and he complains of sleeplessness, desperation, and a contact list of "useless names." In sonnet 5 he admires a beautiful go-go dancer at a nightclub. Incongruously, the two become an item, and the poet feels flattered to gad about with such a handsome piece of "arm-candy." But in the end, he dismisses the dancer as trivial and insipid: despite his good looks, there's no depth behind his beady black eyes. Already in sonnets 12 and 13, he consigns him to the past. In the following poem, he undergoes a sudden epiphany at the supermarket, where he discovers his new idol in the delicatessen section. He observes his graceful gestures as he plies his trade, and lists all the foods he buys from him. As the clerk hands the poet his purchases in a sack, it is the poet he has "bagged." From now on, the irresistible grocer is the poet's passion, and his eventual partner in life.

Now the menu is set for a smorgasbord of food metaphors, which richly garnish the remaining sonnets. Shakespeare's plays often allude to popular dishes in Elizabethan England; yet his poems contain nothing similar, probably because sonnets were still considered a "noble" verse-form. Sonnet 75 comes closest, but it is generic "love-food" for which the poet longs. For his part, Simonelli multiplies the culinary motifs with a profusion and relish that will strike many readers as quintessentially Italian. From the beginning, the "good lover" is associated with mortadella, chicken in aspic, pancetta, cheese, and salami. Returning the favor, in sonnet 15 the lover dreams of the poet as a meal being broiled by the sun, a breaded turkey breast with potato croquettes.

Should they make love on the fantasy beach, or in the actual kitchen? In 16, the lover whets his tooth on the poet's neck while he simmers in the shower. The poet consumes the lover as a soft puree in 17, while the lover swallows the ill-tempered poet like a "poison berry." In 19, he lays his poems like eggs, and in 22 their love-making is depicted as a feast, incessantly renewed by their gluttony. In the final sonnet, they exchange their marital vows over biscotti and tea.

The go-go dancer's emblem is a python he keeps in a case; like his pet serpent, the "gloomy hunk" writhes and glitters in his disco cage. But his outward beauty is only a vacuous husk, a strobe-light mirage. The fact that the grocer's physical features are never described suggests that his inner qualities—affection, patience, and fidelity—take precedence over his appearance. The poet's union with him is a marriage made in heaven, as the final verses of *Will* playfully attest. Still, Simonelli never places "spiritual virtues" above the immediacy of erotic pleasure. If anything, the wanton details that abound in the second half of his sonnet cycle are even more explicit than in the first. Like Shakespeare—and unlike his idealizing predecessors in the earlier Petrarchist canon—Simonelli revindicates the sensual verve and downright bawdiness of love.

*
* *

My translation of *Will: 24 Sonnets* first appeared in 2022 as an online chapbook in the Mudlark series. In preparing this print version for Spuyten Duyvil, I discovered that Simonelli had written ten unpublished sonnets in the same style. Though contemporary to the others, they were not included in the Italian original of *Will* (2009). I have added them to the present book, because they complement the main cycle in their verse-form and metrics, even if their themes seem to depart from its two-lover scheme—and from the Shakespearean model in general. Accordingly, this collection of thirty-four poems is the first complete edition of Simonelli's amatory sonnets in both Italian and English.

I use the phrase "seem to depart" advisedly, since the ten new sonnets often echo *Will* and Shakespeare himself by contrast, variation, or nuanced parallels. Simonelli's sonnet 4 is a clear-cut parody of Shakespeare's sonnet 18, "Shall I compare thee to a summer's day?" Here the radiant weather turns foul, and anti-Petrarchist motifs subvert the sunny adoration of the English poem. In fact, Shakespeare himself uses a similar technique to undermine the "fair young man" at the end of his sequence. Sonnets 1 and 3 reprise the culinary comparisons of *Will*, just as 5, 6, 7, and 9 might be said to expand the gallery of conquests at the beginning of Simonelli's cycle. Though mournfully, Shakespeare also insists on the many "trophies" of his former loves in sonnet 31.

Simonelli's sonnet 2 takes up *Will's* recurring motif of love as a pathological affliction, now spreading it from the lover to the beloved, fused inextricably. The topos of passion as a sickness is generic to Petrarchist poetry throughout the centuries, and Shakespeare is no exception. Simonelli emphasizes his allegiance to the tradition by many deft details, such as the archaic verb-form "porìa" in line 2 of sonnet 6. He again follows his precursor's example in sonnet 3, where he imagines himself as a wizened old man, bereft of youthful potency. His sonnet 8 remotely evokes the "increase sonnets" at the outset of Shakespeare's cycle, which sagely counsel the young man on his coming of age. Finally, Simonelli's drastic vision of nuclear disaster in sonnet 10—while it obviously lacks any precedent in Shakespeare's time— revisits the eternal union of the spouses at the close of *Will*.

And yet, it would be out of keeping to end this whimsical collection on such a catastrophic chord. Simonelli's sonnets trace a cautiously optimistic tale of love fulfilled. By "rewriting" Shakespeare in a contemporary Tuscan mode, he has served up a repast of pungent humor and bittersweet irony. With the author's approval, I have appended a coda that leaves the sonnet-form behind; it affords a parting glimpse of what the future may hold for *Will's* newlyweds. The perspective shifts to the voyeurism of a ghost, who naively deflates her own outdated prejudices. Come what "will," we still hope that love "will" triumph over every obstacle, whether inner or outer—even in an age of uncertainty. This is the overriding message of Simonelli's wittily amorous work.

—Hoyt Rogers

WILL: *24 SONNETS*

Will, come voglia, desiderio. Come il malizioso nomignolo con cui, nei suoi sonetti, Shakespeare chiamava sé stesso e il suo fair friend. Will, come un verbo al futuro che, in un'epoca in cui anche i rapporti umani sono precari, appare sempre più incerto, oscillante, basculante.

Will, like wish, desire. Like the naughty nickname Shakespeare gave to himself and his fair friend in his sonnets. Will, like a verb in the future tense—which, in an era when human relationships are also precarious, appears more and more uncertain, wobbly, wavering.

1

Tuffato nella fonte di Narciso
m'innamoravo solo di riflessi.
Ogni tratto somatico del viso
scompariva all'arrivo degli amplessi
che consumavo inevitabilmente
proiettando l'immagine di me
dentro un corpo diverso ma presente
che non mi richiedeva alcun perché.
Ed era naturale quello sdarsi
cercando senza sosta il sottoporsi
ad un teatro privo di catarsi
che il cuore sceneggiava di rimorsi.
    Ed ancora da fulmine colpito
    correvo dietro un tipo benvestito.

Narcissus, I'd plunge into a pool,
in love with my reflections alone.
Each distinctive feature of the face
would fade once intercourse began.
The sex I unavoidably devoured
engraved the image of myself
on a different body, yet still there,
which never asked me to say why.
This giving-in was only natural,
the restless impulse to submit
to a theatre without catharsis,
staged by my remorseful heart.
    And love-struck at first sight again,
    I hotly pursued a well-dressed guy.

2

Il sonno che m'umilia giornalmente,
quel sonno non dormito, speso invano
perlustrando boscaglie nella mente,
comatoso, in trip, steso sul divano,
ad occhi aperti, nel farneticare,
da molta caffeina sostenuto
sul tema dell'amore e del variare
gridando «Al lupo! Al lupo! Aiuto! Aiuto!»
Ché nulla nella veglia è chiara cosa
se la palpebra cala eppur s'ostina
a rimaner di scatto aperta in posa
qual tonda biglia, sferica pallina.
  Sveglio, veglio il dilemma maledetto.
  E domani? Domani che mi metto?

Humiliating sleep, a sleep not slept
that keeps me scouring every day
through all my mental underbrush,
in a trippy daze on my sofa-bed,
my eyes pried open by caffeine
as I rant and rave upon the theme
of love and its vagaries, crying
"Wolf! Wolf! Oh help me please!"
Nothing when I wake is clear at all
if my eyelids droop but still persist
in snapping back to their usual pose
over rounded marbles, spherical balls.
    Waking up, I wake to the same damn bind.
    And tomorrow? Then what pills will I pop?

3

Trabocca la rubrica, nomi vani,
una folla di numeri inattivi
mobili cellulari interurbani
di volto e di sembianza e d'occhi privi,
serbate prede, incontri promettenti
fermati in morte voci prevedibili
d'apparati perennemente spenti
d'utenti assenti sempre irraggiungibili.
Sintetica s'allarga la memoria,
intorno a me si stringe lo schedario.
La solita dannata e mesta storia:
finito lo spettacolo, sipario:
  l'attore dopo l'ultima intervista
  solo, senza alcun coprotagonista.

My contact list brims over with useless
names, tons of numbers out of service,
mobile phones, long-distance cells
devoid of faces and features and eyes,
saved-up prey, promising hookups
dead in their tracks, voices foregone
from gizmos eternally switched off
by absent users, always unreachable.
As artificial memory extends,
its filing systems hem me in.
The usual blasted, rueful tale:
show's over, the curtain falls.
    After his last interview, the actor's
    alone; his co-stars have vamoosed.

4

Parcheggia la tua bocca sulla mia.
Estrai da portafoglio monetina.
Rimetti in moto. Non cambiar corsia.
Sicuro d'aver messo la benzina?
Codesto tuo motore appar truccato.
Allaccia oppure slaccia le cinture.
Ribaltami qual camion cappottato.
Arresta. Sosta. Poi riparti pure.
Mille miglia e chilometri e raccordi.
Un corpo come casa cantoniera.
Col finestrino aperto qui m'abbordi,
con pantaloni jeans e canottiera.
  Io mi dedico anonimo ad un vizio
  ammissibile in area di servizio.

Park your mouth on top of mine.
Take a little coin from your wallet.
Rev up again. Don't change lanes.
You sure your tank's full of gas?
Looks like your motor's souped-up.
Buckle the seat-belts; unbuckle them.
Flip me over like an upturned truck.
Stop. Idle a while. Then start again.
Thousands of miles and access ramps.
A body like a road-worker's house.
You veer close to me in a tank-top
and jeans, your window open wide.
   Anonymous, I get down to work
   on a vice this service-area allows.

5

Oh cubista che unto ti dimeni
in questa disco inferno per maschietti:
cosa pretendi da me? Che t'aspetti?
Attendi che di dollari mi sveni?
Guardar e non toccar la merce esposta.
Mi guardi con gli occhioni tipo manga.
Ti riguardo e desidero il tuo tanga.
E poi mi dici che l'amore costa.
Lo fai apposta? No tengo dinero!
Se solo fosse vero questo sogno
ricoprirei di dindi il tuo bisogno
baciandoti il baffetto da sparviero...
　　Vorrei aver di spiccioli un bel sacco
　　da scaricarti il peso dentro il pacco.

Oh oiled-up go-go boy who bumps,
grinds, in this disco-hell for queens:
Fess up! What do you expect from me?
Dollars? Do you want to bleed me dry?
Look at the merchandise, don't touch:
you fix your eyes on me like a manga.
I stare back, and lust for your tanga.
Then you tell me that love will cost.
Is this on purpose? No tengo dinero!
If only my dream would come true,
I'd shower you with wads of dough,
kissing your handle-bar moustache...
    I'd like to have a big pile of change
    to unload that weight in your package.

6

Un pitone tenevi in una teca.
Portavi, agli occhi, lenti colorate.
Facevi il ballerino in discoteca.
Studiando ingegneria le tue giornate
trascorrevano a Pisa tali e quali
a quelle che a Firenze conducevo.
Chiedevi di comprarti dei regali.
Non mi volevi bene, lo sapevo,
ma molto mi piaceva il tuo fornirmi
un accompagnamento assai vistoso.
A letto non riuscivo a divertirmi.
Ma frequentando te, bel tenebroso
  compresi che l'estetica non basta
  a trasformare in pane muta pasta.

You kept a python inside a theca,
wore colored lenses on your eyes.
You go-go danced at a discotheque.
A student engineer, you whiled
away your days in Pisa just as I,
in Florence, was spending mine.
You asked me to buy you gifts.
You didn't love me, that I knew.
But I adored the arm-candy glitz
you granted me when we went out.
In bed I never managed to have fun.
Frequenting you, my gloomy hunk,
    I grasped that beauty won't suffice
    to bake wordless dough into bread.

7

Non c'è riparo dalle tue chiamate
dagli esse emme esse inaciditi
in cui affondo in onde elettrizzate
senza filo sui crediti finiti.
La batteria schiantata, non ho presa
a cui ricaricar il cor deriso.
Io sogno una chiamata che inattesa
si manifesti con sonoro avviso
che squilli di campane, suoneria,
che la parola sia più forte e chiara
che non sia bara la segreteria
di vecchia voce che l'amor dichiara.
   Per avere un amore sì perfetto
   non basta premer tasto cancelletto.

There's no refuge from your calls,
from your text sms's turning sour
where I founder in electric waves
on wireless credit that's run out.
Battery smashed, I have no plug
to recharge my derided heart.
I dream of an unexpected ring
that would reverberate for me,
chiming like bells, like a clarion
of words resounding loud and clear
—and not a message-service tomb
for a worn voice declaring its love.

   For such a perfect love it's not
   enough to press the cancel key.

8

La somma dei miei mali opprime il plesso
ostruendo le vene e poi l'arterie;
questo male la testa ha compromesso,
ridotta in condizione più che serie.
Il sesso è quella cosa ch'apre e chiude
il respiro, il coraggio addormentato
che, sveglio, salta, corre e non delude
qual cucciolo di cane appena nato.
Ma quando poi si fa licantropia,
mensile vocazione a distruzione
allarme accende, pulsa rossa spia
a segnalar di mente distrazione.

  Non è bussola, questo strano cuore,
  ma timer, ordigno, contatore.

Mounting ailments knot my gut;
they clog my veins and arteries;
the aches that sabotage my head
don't burst, they're steady-state.
Sex is a valve that opens and shuts
the breath, sparking our sleepy zest
to skip and gambol with delight,
frisky as a newborn puppy-dog.
But when it morphs into a werewolf,
bent on bloody mayhem every month,
then it triggers our alarms: red lights
signal that our mind is now deranged.
  This weird heart isn't a compass
  but a bomb, its timer ticking down.

9

Ti risplende di glitter tutto il torso
anchéggi e ti dimeni in luce strobo,
spaccacuori senz'ombra di rimorso
riflesso arcobaleno sotto il globo
che scintillando ruota sulla pista
in un'orbita accesa di faville.
Taciturno ed efebico egoista:
trent'anni e fai ancora l'imbecille,
fatato fatalone del locale
che veste solamente D&G,
in cerca d'un rapporto che sessuale
t'appaghi immantinente. Signorsì:
  ti servirebbe un tipo autoritario
  ariete o toro oppure dell'acquario.

Your entire torso glints with glitter;
in strobe-lights, you wiggle and twist.
Below the scintillating globe, spinning
above the dancers with orbiting sparks,
you shed a rainbow gleam. You break
our hearts without a shadow of remorse.
Self-centered and tight-lipped ephebe,
at thirty you're still acting like a fool:
the enchanted heartthrob of the club,
who never wears anything but D&G.
You're on the prowl for a sex-mate
who'll gratify you instantly. Yessir:
    you need some bossy guy, an Aries
    or a Taurus—or maybe an Aquarius.

10

Foriera è luna piena di collassi
di nervi che sfilacciano di guasti
che bisogna aspettare che mi passi
che con me non toccare certi tasti
che spesso vado in palla, do di matto
che ti urlo e ti caccio via di casa
ti faccio doccia fredda di soppiatto
a parolacce ch'ho la testa invasa
di sanguinarie scene di delitti.
Sono esaurito e stanco, son depresso
e tu mi neghi, neghi quei diritti
di coccole e carezze e poi di sesso
 ché quando perdo staffe di ragione
 non chiedo dell'amore l'esenzione.

The full moon is a harbinger of nerves
collapsing, fraying into cranky moods.
You need to wait for them to pass,
not harp on your hackneyed tunes:
how often I get confused, go ballistic;
or how I shout and show you the door,
treat you to frigid showers of curses
on the sly; or how my head is packed
with scenes of blood-stained crimes.
I'm blotto, I'm fagged, I'm depressed;
yet you deny me, you deny my rights
to cuddles and hugs, and then to sex:
    but when my mind has lost its grip,
    I don't ask you to throw love out.

11

Pace non v'è in questo calumet.
Esitando m'aspiro un altro tiro.
Ridiamo insieme stesi sul parquet.
L'accendiamo? Sì. Ora. Un altro giro.
Un'altra corsa. Giostra, l'intelletto
con sostanza illegale oror dopato
accende in corpo elettrico diletto:
bisogno di slacciar ciò che attillato
ancora i fianchi fascia per pudore.
Liberato da questo perizoma
dimostri raddoppiato il tuo vigore.
Oh, erboso e fiorito e tosto aroma!
  Nonostante la nebbia nell'ambiente
  io ti piaccio davvero. È evidente.

There's no peace in this pipe.
I hesitate; I take another toke.
We laugh together, sprawled on the floor.
Should we light up? Yes. Now. Another
round, another rush. The mind, doped
by an illegal substance, is a circus ride:
in the body, an electric pleasure soars.
We have to loosen what still binds
the hips so tightly out of modesty.
Freed from that G-string, you parade
your oomph with a redoubled vim.
Oh, grassy and floral and toasty scent!
  Despite this fog in the ambient air,
  you're really into me. It's obvious.

12

Poco resta di te nei miei discorsi,
ermetici vasetti di veleno;
riga sul collo: mangiami di morsi!
Trangugiami. Lo stomaco sia pieno
oggetto di gastrite e di bugie
modulate su pessima frequenza,
apatiche ed insulse litanie
scoppiate da quel vuoto di giacenza
sul tuo cervello molle di pensieri
tarato d'ignoranza, interferenza.
Abbassi gli occhi? Quei pallini neri,
indici della scarsa intelligenza
   non sono specchi d'anima profonda.
   Oh! Quanto è masochista chi c'affonda!

Little of you remains in my chats—
poison stored up in vials, airtight.
Your collar reads: Eat me in bites!
Gobble me up. Stuff your belly
chock-full with gastritis and lies,
modulated at a horrendous pitch,
litanies drab and inane that crackle
and pop from the vacant storage
in your low-watt brain, unhinged
by ignorance, static interference.
You lower your eyes? Those black
beads, signs of your feeble intellect,
   are hardly mirrors of a deeper soul.
   Oh! Only masochists founder there!

13

Noi siamo i tasti ch'egli percuotea,
l'ottico mouse sul suo tappetino,
il modem che trasmise l'epopea
di quel cuore ridotto un moncherino.
A te ci presentiam giacché siam stanchi
di produrre una lagna digitale
compressa in documenti Word. Gli manchi.
Lo sa ch'è stato errore madornale
comportarsi così, da deficiente.
Ormai da tempo sconta il suo peccato.
Noi ti preghiamo d'essere clemente.
Scorda il passato. Ciò ch'è stato è stato.
    Siamo certi che ti dedicherà,
    tramite radio Ne me quitte pas.

We're the keys that he strikes,
the optical mouse on his pad,
the modem that sent the epic tale
of his heart whittled down to a stub.
We hand him to you; we're fed up
with producing his digital laments,
compressed into Word documents.
He misses you. He knows it was a huge
mistake to behave like such an idiot.
Now he's atoned for his sin, long ago.
We implore you, show mercy to him.
Forget about the past. What was, was.
   We have no doubt that over the radio
   he'll dedicate to you "Ne me quitte pas."

14

Servi gastronomia alla Coop.
Non prosciutto né pollo in gelatina
m'accende nella gola gran falò
ma la mano ch'affetta sopraffina
quell'unta, grassa, dolce mortadella,
che esperta taglia forte la cotenna
che dentro al foglio stende e poi modella
la fetta d'affettato e con la penna
il subtotale segna soppesando
la gravità di questa cotoletta.
Non è cibo che vado comprando
né salame, formaggio oppur pancetta.
    Mentre mi porgi un etto d'insaccato
    molto di te mi sono infatuato.

You man the Coop's delicatessen.
Not prosciutto nor chicken in aspic
kindles a bonfire in my throat
but your hand, slicing wafer-thin
that sweet, oily, fatty mortadella,
trimming its rind with forceful skill,
laying it out on paper, then shaping
the array of meat, and with a pen
noting the subtotal as you gauge
the cold-cut's weight. It's not food
that I am purchasing: not salami,
not cheese—and not pancetta, either.
   As you hand me a sack with a hundred
grams, it's lovesick me you've bagged.

15

Ritorni dal lavoro stanco morto,
ti stendi a letto in cerca di riposo
e salpi allora verso un altro porto
in un viaggio mentale e non costoso.
A nuoto mi raggiungi sulla spiaggia,
indosso un tanga nero e striminzito.
Il sale della pelle il sole assaggia.
M'abbronzo dalla fronte all'infradito.
Mi sogni disponibile, accaldato.
Ti chiedi se croccante è la mia pelle.
Un petto di tacchino già impanato,
contorno di patate fritte a stelle.
    Hai fame di me, hai l'acquolina.
    Ma lo facciamo in spiaggia od in cucina?

Dead tired, you come back from work,
stretch out on the bed in search of rest,
and then set sail towards another port
in a mental voyage that's low in cost.
You swim to meet me on the beach;
I'm wearing a tanga, skimpy and black.
The sun samples the salt on my skin.
I tan from my forehead to my thongs.
You dream of me, available and hot.
You wonder whether my skin is crisp.
A breaded turkey breast, garnished
with star-shaped potato croquettes.
    Your mouth waters; you're starved for me.
    Do we do it in the kitchen or on the beach?

16

Feroce il dente aguzzi sul mio collo
sotto una doccia calda ma non troppo.
Sarà questo succhiotto un francobollo
per rispedirmi a te senza l'intoppo
di carta e busta con i cuoricini:
messaggio che ti giunge inaspettato,
che scorre sotto gli occhi tuoi bambini,
prodotto manuale, artigianato
di cui tu sai che vado molto fiero.
Lo prendo in mano e scuoto ad ogni rima
questo lapis che schizza inchiostro nero
con te scrivendo, o dopo, oppure prima,
  insomma, prolungandomi nel petto
  l'albume del piacer ch'avemmo a letto.

You whet your fierce tooth on my neck
under a shower not scalding, though hot.
Could this hickey be a postage stamp
to send me back to you, minus the hitch
of an envelope and card with tiny hearts?
An unexpected message you receive,
that flows before your childlike eyes—
a handicraft the workmanship of which,
as you must know, swells me with pride.
I take hold of it and jiggle at every rhyme
this pen that squirts black ink while I write
with you—or later, to sum up, if not before,

I expand the album within my heart
of those pleasures we pursue in bed.

17

Ma tu come mi vedi? Crederesti
che dopo le parole sono pappa
di latte zuccherato? Mi vedresti
pan bagnato che bolle sotto cappa,
sopra l'azzurro fuoco di cucina?
Chi mi difenderà dalla tua bocca
che s'apre tutta aspersa d'acquolina
qual pesce rosso che ad un'esca abbocca?
Molle purè, ti scivolo per gola
ti cucio le budella col ricamo
a rilegare la vetusta fola
nel libro che contien l'amore e l'amo.
  O visione famelica gustosa:
  tu m'inghiotti qual bacca velenosa.

But you, how do you see me? Could you
believe, after my words, that I'm a mush
of sugary milk? Or think of me as bread,
soaked and boiling beneath the hood
of a kitchen range, atop its bluish fire?
Who'll defend me from your watering
mouth that opens wide, like a goldfish
greedily swimming to gulp the bait?
A soft puree, I slide down your throat.
I stitch your innards with embroidery
to bind that ancient page once more
into the book containing love and lure.

    O ravenous vision, yet so delectable:
you swallow me like a poison berry.

18

I miei musi son musi artificiali
desideri che saltano la corda,
gatti randagi senza gli stivali
che m'assalgono – barbari – in un'orda
che mi sorprende in trance addormentato
mentre rimiro un qualche tipo in spiaggia.
Io scrivo del futuro e del passato
immaginando un'orgia che selvaggia
non avviene che dentro la mia mente.
Oppur vagheggio mèmore di quando
in un'era distante dal presente
andavo per la strada sculettando
   cercando in altrui sguardo l'attenzione.
   Poi l'ho trovata. Quale frustrazione…

My male muses are artificial,
desires that keep jumping rope,
a horde of pusses-without-boots,
strays who assail me—the hooligans.
They startle me, drowsing in a trance
while I cruise some guy on the beach.
I write of the future and the past;
I imagine a wild orgy that occurs
nowhere but within my own mind.
Or else I yearn, recalling when—
in a time so distant from today—
I strutted down the street, seeking
    attention from somebody's gaze.
    Then I found it. What frustration...

19

L'attitudine della portinaia –
la mia caratteristica primaria:
una gallina, ascolto dentro l'aia
tutto il gossip che pigola nell'aria
il cuore, quel galletto starnazzante
che mi feconda uova nella testa.
Le depongo su carta, noncurante
dell'inchiostro che cola nella cesta.
Divulgo il mio piacer al condominio
pettegolo d'amor che chiacchierando
rende anche me di pubblico dominio
voce che mi sussurra di rimando
    notizia del palazzo, del pollaio.
    Il guscio rotto dentro un altro guaio.

The concierge's attitude—this
is my character trait number one.
A hen in the barnyard, I overhear
all the gossip that's crowed abroad
by the heart, that flapping rooster
who fertilizes eggs within my head.
I lay them on paper, unconcerned
by the ink that seeps into the basket.
I cluck about my pleasure to the condo,
prattle about my love, and my chatter
shunts me too into the public domain—
rumors that whisper back to me in turn
 news of the building, the chicken coop.
 A broken eggshell there: another mess

20

Ancora mi masturbo amico mio,
faccio di me strumento d'entropia.
Ritengo di non credere nel dio
assolutista. Oh! Che fantasia
nascondere l'impenitente cuore
contro una porta chiusa malamente!
Origlia sempre, quel registratore
buono ad intercettar sovente
un losco mormorio della coscienza
facitore di rime demodé.
Fuorilegge la bianca mia semenza
ottunde i sensi. Ma chissà perché
  non si rassegna calma nelle membra
  insulsa forma che umile non sembra.

I still masturbate, my friend: I make
myself into an instrument of entropy.
I retain my disbelief in the absolutist
god. Oh! What a fantasy it is
to hide my impenitent heart
behind a door that's left ajar!
It still eavesdrops, that recorder,
so adept at often intercepting
a shifty murmur of the mind,
the molder of outmoded rhymes.
Renegade, my pearly seed blunts
my senses. Yet perhaps because
    it isn't calm, resigned amid my limbs,
     it seems a mild, but not humble shape.

21

Potremmo divertirci, noi, stasera,
eiaculando insieme, parimenti,
ripassando di nuovo la frontiera
talvolta aperta a sensi differenti.
Occorre il desiderio. Le parole
mi mastican qual gomma masticata.
Muovendo sul parquet le dure suole
annaspo dentro un'ansia spalancata.
Solo verso le dieci ti fai vivo,
ormai distrutto da duro lavoro.
Liquori non ne vuoi. L'aperitivo
insisto che tu beva, oh mio bel toro!
   «Salute!» dici. E cadi sul divano
   alcolico dormiente mio vulcano.

We'll be able to have fun tonight,
we two, ejaculating equally as one,
crossing that frontier again, open
to sensations that sometimes change.
Desire occurs. Words chew on me
like chewing gum already chewed.
Clacking my leather soles on the wood
parquet, I flail inside with flaring angst.
Not till ten or so do you show up,
wasted by now from heavy work.
Liquor, you'll have none. But I still insist
you drink a cocktail, my handsome bull!
    "Cheers!" you say. And fall on the sofa—
    my plastered volcano, dormant for now.

22

A frutta siamo giunti – dici – e dopo?
Appare terminato il gran menù.
Ma sappi ch'io ti son di verbo cuoco
e non intendo smetterla, se tu
sazio ti senti d'indigesto cranio
azzanna e fai boccon del cuore, morso,
giacché ce l'ho più duro del titanio
quel muscolo che plasma mette in corso.
Rigettami e rivomita me pasto
sì come fossi afflitto in bulimia:
comincia un nuovo pranzo ancor più vasto
ed abbi più pietà, pietanza mia.
　　Ti prego riprendiamo quel bagordo
　　　di cui son ghiotto e molto, avido, ingordo.

We've reached the fruit course, you say—
and now? The main menu's done, it seems.
But bear in mind that I'm your verbal chef,
and I'm not inclined to leave off. If you
feel stuffed with my brain, hard to digest,
chomp on my heart as a mouthful, a bite—
all the more, since my plasma-pumping
muscle has become stiffer than titanium.
Regurgitate me like a meal, throw up
as if you're overmastered by bulimia.
Start a new and even bigger lunch,
and dish out more mercy, my dish.
   I beg you, let's begin our frolics again.
   For them I hunger, unsated as a glutton

23

Un futuro di mille gigabyte
attende la cartella delle foto
e le immagini che mi scatterai –
un flash che fisserà in un immoto
ritratto realista quei momenti
di te e di me durante gite al mare
oppure dentro un altro degli ambienti
che tu deciderai d'immortalare.
Nello storaggio sta riproduzione
di ciò che appare certo all'occhio umano
ma non c'è spazio per quell'emozione
che ogni volta compare nella mano
   il nostro esser, scatto dopo scatto
   non più soli bensì coppia di fatto.

A future of a thousand gigabytes
awaits the folder of our photos
and the images you'll snap of us
in flashes that immovably arrest
realist portraits of me and you:
those outings to the seaside,
or to any other backdrop you
have decided to immortalize.
In that storage, what seems true
to the human eye is reproduced;
but there's no space for the thrill
that floods our hands every time:
    our life as a common-law couple,
    no longer alone, in shot after shot.

24

Il Vaticano dice di non farlo.
Vuol dir che non avremo cerimonia.
Ma quello Stato che moneta conia
il nostro patto, amor, non può disfarlo.
Ci unimmo un pomeriggio nel salotto,
sfiorandoci le mani, per merenda.
«Di tue ferite io sarò la benda»
promettemmo mangiandoci un biscotto.
In fondo non vogliamo un matrimonio.
Ci basta un bacio da scambiarci al sole,
un avvenir di giorni come prole.
È questa la ricchezza, il patrimonio.
   (Chi ci dice che quelli con le ali
   non siano anche loro omosessuali?)

The Vatican tells us not to do it:
no wedding for us, that means.
But this State that mints the coins,
my love, cannot dissolve our pact.
Joined together for a tea-time snack
in the sitting-room, we touch hands.
As we munch a cookie, we promise:
"I'll be the bandage for your wounds."
At bottom, we don't want a marriage.
Sharing a kiss in the sun is enough:
for our offspring, our future of days.
This indeed is our fortune, our wealth.
   (Who says they're not queers as well,
    those beings up there with the wings?)

10 More Sonnets

1

Pezzo di manzo. Sudo. Ho l'acquolina.
Erotico cinghiale al pepe rosa...
Rigiro e frollo carne qui in cucina.
Salsiccia di suino. Clamorosa.
Inutile impanarti e farti a fette,
mangiarti gli arti, farne una poltiglia:
ormai ho terminato le ricette.
Neppure arrosto, in forno o sulla griglia.
Eppure stai cuocendo nel tuo brodo.
Bollendo espelli un grasso che depura,
rilasci un lardo dove annego e godo,
un vasto pasto che la fame cura.
  Non ti divorerò cotto, ma crudo.
  Oppure al dente. Basta che sia nudo.

A hunk of beef: I sweat, mouth watering.
This pink-pepper boar, erotic as can be...
In my kitchen, I spit-roast curing meat.
Pork sausage. It's totally over the top.
No use breading you or slicing you up,
gnawing your limbs, dicing you to mush:
from now on, my recipes are bunk.
Not even braised, baked, or grilled.
And yet, you simmer in your broth.
Boiling, you extrude a fat that purifies,
release a lard that drowns me in bliss,
a stupendous, hunger-healing feast.

   I won't devour you cooked, but raw.
   Or else al dente. Just so you're nude.

2

L'azienda sanitaria se ne frega
non controlla la nostra epidemia,
l'infermità pulsante che ci lega
invalidi in medesima corsia:
un herpes che c'arrossa dall'interno,
un virus che patogeno ci guasta.
Lo spasmo partirà sotto lo sterno
schiacciandoci la vena cava e vasta.
Tossicomani in crisi d'astinenza
cronicamente fusi qual siamesi
esigiamo reciproca assistenza.
Dall'incidente non uscimmo illesi.
   Urgente si richiede trasfusione.
   Un cuore nuovo, dopo amputazione.

Public Health doesn't give a damn
if our epidemic's under control—
the throbbing malady that binds
our two infirmities as they spike.
A herpes that reddens from within,
a viral pathogen that lays us waste.
Below the sternum, the spasm starts,
then triggers the huge, hollow vein.
Addicts under withdrawal pains,
chronically fused like Siamese twins,
we demand some reciprocal help.
We won't come out of this unharmed.
    A transfusion is urgently required.
    After amputation, a brand-new heart.

3

Guance come cartine autostradali
i giorni incideranno sul mio viso.
Rughe cupe. Dovrò portar gli occhiali.
Invecchierò così, all'improvviso,
mutando una mattina in un rottame
oppure (oddio! Presagio d'agonia!)
nuotando a dorso in fetido liquame,
trascorrerò vecchiaia a geriatria?
Ignoro se sia meglio in vampa spiccia
girare i tacchi, andarsene fra i più
rispetto a un afflosciarsi della ciccia
estesa in lungo tempo, un barbecue
  che sfrigolando fonde all'infinito
  opulento organismo abbrustolito.

Cheeks that resemble highway maps:
on my face, the days will take their toll.
Deep wrinkles. I'll need to wear glasses.
Like that, all of a sudden, I'll grow old—
transformed one morning into a wreck?
Or else (oh God, what dire foreboding!)
I'll spend my twilight in a geriatric ward,
swimming backstroke in a putrid mess?
I don't know if it's better to turn tail
in a searing flame, or leave the scene
with utmost respect, as the grilled
flab buckles over time, a sizzled
   barbecue that softens to the max,
   an organism sumptuously broiled.

4

Oh, no, non t'assomiglia un dì d'estate,
piuttosto buia notte tempestosa,
mattina d'abbondanti nevicate.
Come gelo, che pioggia prende in sposa,
in grandine mutando vai quel chicco
ch'è seme di frumento prosperoso.
Ti raffreddi, l'umore crolla a picco,
odioso, più nervoso, permaloso.
Subisco abbassamento di passione:
il barometro – bussola impazzita
m'uncina qual balena ad un arpione.
Oh inclemente Tempo, in questa gita
   rovesci un uragano di pantano
   qual fusse guano su volto silvano.

No, I can't compare you to a summer's day.
Instead, you're like a somber, stormy night,
a morning blizzard with banked-up slush.
You're like a frost that weds itself to rain:
you mutate into hail whatever kernels
might've sown the seed of hardy wheat.
You turn cold, your mood goes bust:
you're hateful, crabby, and on edge.
I suffer as passion declines, a droop
in the barometer: that barmy compass
hooks me like a whale to a harpoon.
Oh inclement Weather, on this jaunt
    you blast with guano the sylvan face,
    a hurricane as mucky as a swamp.

5

"Ciao, grazie", mi dici, ché t'ho dato
solo una sigaretta mentre al parco
portavi a spasso il cane. M'hai guardato
e poi m'hai detto che ti chiami Marco
e che sei a Firenze di passaggio.
La tua cresta bordeaux è divertente.
Ma sei di carne oppure sei miraggio?
La faccia di briccone impenitente
impertinente tace e fissa molto.
Sei fiore punkabbestia nel giardino
sbocciato presto, subito raccolto.
"Andiamo al bar, ti compro un tramezzino".
    Ma, mentre mangi, nulla mi racconti
    del tuo vagar, del viver sotto i ponti.

"Hey, thanks," you tell me, who've only
given you a cigarette, while you walked
your dog in the park. You looked at me
and then you said Marco is your name;
in Florence, you're just passing through.
Your burgundy mohawk is a lot of fun.
But are you flesh and blood, or a mirage?
You have a lowlife's unrepentant mug;
you shut up brazenly and stare a bunch.
In the garden, you're a gutter-punk bloom:
quick to blossom, you're rapidly picked.
"Let's go to the bar, I'll buy you a sandwich."
But as you munch, you don't say jack
about your hobo life, a bridge for a roof.

6

Quelle parti di te che stanno sotto
non si porìa ridirle con parole:
un pugno vero in faccia, un bel cazzotto
per me che mi riscaldo sotto il sole,
per me che piccoletto ti rimiro
e non m'accodo al coro che di te
l'elogio tutto tesse in un sospiro.
O tu bello e impossibile, perché?
Com'è che quando parli con qualcuno
a malapena spìccichi due frasi?
Superdotata bestia del raduno
il moto del cervello muti in stasi.
    Tu bugiardo consiglio per gli acquisti
    muto oratòr nel campo di nudisti.

Those parts of you down there below
can't be spelled out in so many words:
a genuine smack in the face, a big dick
as the sun makes me hot—just for me,
for little old me. Sure, I admire you,
but don't queue up to swell the choir
that weaves your praises with a sigh.
Hunk, you're impossible—but why?
When you talk with someone, how come
you can barely spare a couple of grunts?
Astride the rally's best-endowed bike,
the motor of your brain stalls and stops.
  Your con man's spiel for purchasers
  is the mute hawker at a nudist camp.

7

Amabile ragazzo, in tuo potere
da giorni sto, stremato nell'attesa;
senza mutande ti voglio vedere
aprire il pacco, prender la sorpresa
che tu nascosta celi fra i tuoi fianchi.
Non dico frasi inutili, lo vedi.
Forse dovrei dirti che mi manchi?
Mi stanchi se per molto non concedi
la tua figura a queste mie pupille
che la Natura affligge da strabismo.
Spogliati. Poi promettimi scintille,
che tutto mi soddisfi il voyeurismo.

   Ecco. Spostati da sinistra a destra.
   Non chiudere, ti prego, la finestra.

Lovable boy, for days I've languished
in your power, exhausted by the wait;
I want to see you shed your underwear,
open the package, show me the surprise
you keep concealed between your thighs.
Got it? I'm not beating around the bush.
Maybe I should whine that I need you?
You'll tucker me out if you deprive
my pupils of your figure much more.
Nature afflicts them with strabismus.
Undress. Then promise me sparks:
satisfy my voyeurism, head to toe.

 There you go. Move from left to right.
 I beseech you, don't close the window.

8

Vedrai che questa strada è differente
ed i lampioni accesi non più quelli
del tuo quartiere accondiscendente
verso di te e verso i tuoi fratelli.
Il grande cambiamento ora imminente
e la gente che non sarà la stessa:
adesso che sei grande e consenziente
puoi scegliere di non andare a messa.
Ma ricordati d'indossare il casco
se esci d'estate a sera in motorino.
Se per caso in un'altra vita nasco
sarò più te e meno malandrino.
  Il mio vicino guardo che solenne
  è diventato or ora maggiorenne.

You'll see that this street is different,
and the lit-up lamps no longer those
of our neighborhood that for years
has indulged your brothers and you.
A momentous change is imminent,
and people will not remain the same:
now that you're a consenting adult,
you can choose not to go to Mass.
But remember to strap on your helmet,
driving your scooter on summer eves.
If perchance I'm born into another life,
I'll be less naughty, and more like you.

   I observe my neighbor who's become
   so serious, now that he's come of age.

9

Non è la California, è la Versilia
ch'accende l'onda, il corpo, abbronzatura
afa di caldo, l'aria di Brasilia
brezza scuote marosi di Natura;
dorata pelle lucida – surfista
affiori fuori l'onda, bianca spuma.
Passeggia gente con la trippa trista
ma tu, felice fiesta che consuma
il boxerino fuxia che tu porti
ricordi quell'origine terrestre
di quando manzo coi capelli corti
non eri ancora anfibio ma pedestre
   principe blu disperso nella favola?
   Ora delfino sopra la tua tavola.

Not California, this is Versilia, fired up
by the breakers, the sun-bronzed body,
the sultriness of heat, an air of Brazil—
by a breeze that ripples Nature's waves,
and by the sheen of golden skin: a surfer,
you emerge from the sea, the white foam.
People saunter by with dreary paunches,
but you're a happy feast that eats away
at the fuchsia boxer-trunks you wear.
Are you reminded of your land-based
origins as a beefcake with trimmed hair,
when you weren't an amphibian as yet,
    but Prince Valiant adrift in a fairytale?
    Now you're a dolphin atop your board.

10

Ho sognato disastri nucleari
esplosioni in centrale radioattiva
cancellarsi di corpi, poi gli altari
eretti in una terra che spariva,
sopravvissuti pochi a ricordare
com'era l'aria prima della polvere
nebulosa che rende pietra il mare,
nessun dio che ci poteva assolvere
salvarci dalla fine, proiettarci
in un altrove dove le promesse
mantenute potessero salvarci
e dar da nuovo seme nuova messe.
    Della sciagura solo unico bene
    l'esser con te, lo starsi accanto, insieme.

I dreamed of nuclear disasters,
explosions in a radioactive plant
annulling bodies, then of altars
we set up on a disappearing earth.
Only a few survivors could recall
what air was like before the cloud
of dust that turns the sea to stone,
with no god who could absolve us
or save us from the end, propel us
to an elsewhere of promises kept
that might redeem us and bestow
fresh seeds for a harvest renewed.
    The only benefit of this catastrophe:
we two are still together, side by side.

A Coda

INQUILINI

Sono morta cadendo dalle scale.
Il piede, l'orlo della vestaglia,
nel volo avevo perso le pantofole.
Atterrai sul tappeto dell'ingresso
e fu solo la mia casa a starmi accanto
tenendomi per mano nel trapasso.
Nel necrologio mi piansero i nipoti,
sette sciacalli smaniosi di incassare
i resti immobiliari della zia.
La casa fu venduta tramite agenzia.

E vennero i facchini per i mobili,
e gli architetti con progetti allucinanti;
un branco d'operai invase queste stanze
poi furono picconi e martelli pneumatici,
macerie di mattoni e cavi sradicati.
Rimasero soltanto i muri esterni:
la facciata era un viso stralunato,
le finestre due orbite svuotate.
Ho assistito a questo scempio
senza dire una parola.

OCCUPANTS

I died by falling down the stairs.
My foot, the hem of my housecoat...
in flight my slippers got lost.
I landed on the entrance mat
and only my home stood me by,
holding my hand at my demise.
In the obit my nephews wept,
seven jackals itching to devour
their auntie's real-estate remains.
An agency promptly sold the house.

Then the movers hauled the furniture away;
the architects unveiled their striking designs.
A pack of workers invaded these rooms,
brandishing jackhammers, picks.
Bricks in a rubble, cables ripped out.
Only the outer walls survived:
the façade was an anguished face;
the windows, sockets with no eyes.
I witnessed all this butchery
and never said a word.

Da allora è una tortura:
un finto stile impero nel salone
e quadri pretenziosi alle pareti
per non dire di questi due ragazzi
con la boria di tangheri arricchiti:
lui con i suoi scatti di rabbia
e l'altro con la voce fastidiosa,
le loro smancerie di baci e lingua
e quelle porcherie che fanno a letto,
un amore a dir poco stomachevole

che non posso evitare di guardare.

Since then, it's been a torture:
the sitting-room, faux-Empire style,
with pompous pictures on the walls—
not to mention those boorish boys
and their nouveau-riche conceit.
One with his outbursts of rage;
the other, his tiresome voice.
Their mushy kisses, sweet-talk
and that filth they do in bed:
to say the least, a repulsive love

I just can't help but watch.

ACKNOWLEDGMENTS

Marco Simonelli's *Will: 24 Sonetti* was originally published in 2009 by Edizioni d'if. In 2022, the English version by Hoyt Rogers, *Will: 24 Sonnets*, appeared as an online chapbook in the Mudlark series. The ten additional sonnets by Simonelli as well as the translation by Rogers are published here for the first time. The poem "Inquilini" appeared in Simonelli's collection *Good Manners* (*Le Buone Maniere*, Valigie Rosse, 2018); the translation by Rogers, "Occupants," was published by the *AGNI* review in 2022.

The author and the translator would like to express their gratitude to all the editors who have supported their work. They owe a new debt of thanks to the publishers at Spuyten Duyvil for bringing the present book to fruition.

MARCO SIMONELLI was born in Florence, where he still lives today. A leading voice in the Italian LGBTQ movement, he defies homophobia with mordant humor. Though still in his forties, he has published a dozen titles. His collection *Will*, winner of the Russo–Mazzacurati prize, is a contemporary take on Shakespeare's sonnets, set in modern Tuscany. His most recent book is *Litania nervosa* (*A Litany of Nerves*), published by Valigie Rosse. For a full bibliography and discussions of his work, please consult the internet.

HOYT ROGERS is an award-winning translator, essayist, poet, and novelist. He has published many books, including a study of Renaissance verse; he has contributed to a wide variety of periodicals and anthologies. His latest works are a poetry collection, *Thresholds* (MadHat Press); the novel *Sailing to Noon* (Spuyten Duyvil), book one of *The Caribbean Trilogy*; and a translation of Yves Bonnefoy's *The Wandering Life* (Seagull Books). For more information, please visit his website, hoytrogers.com.

www.ingramcontent.com/pod-product-compliance
Lightning Source LLC
Chambersburg PA
CBHW031448120626
46545CB00006B/2602